This Is a Let's-Read-and-Find-Out Science Book®
Revised Edition

Ducks Don't Get Wet

by Augusta Goldin

illustrated by Leonard Kessler

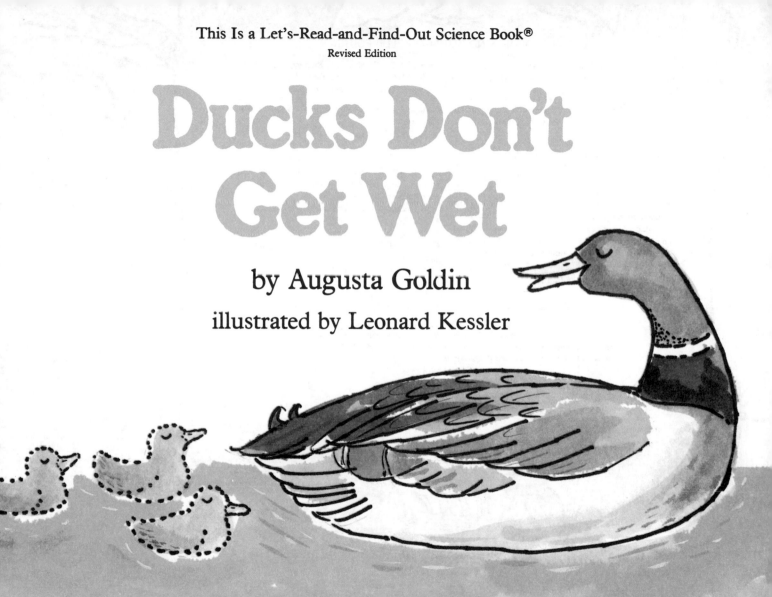

THOMAS Y. CROWELL   NEW YORK

LET'S READ-AND-FIND-OUT BOOK CLUB EDITION

The *Let's-Read-and-Find-Out Science Book* series was originated by Dr. Franklyn M. Branley, Astronomer Emeritus and former Chairman of the American Museum–Hayden Planetarium, and was formerly co-edited by him and Dr. Roma Gans, Professor Emeritus of Childhood Education, Teachers College, Columbia University.

Library of Congress Cataloging-in-Publication Data
Goldin, Augusta R.
    Ducks don't get wet.

    (A Let's-read-and-find-out science book)
    Summary: Describes the habits and behavior of ducks, emphasizing the physical characteristics which prevent their getting wet.
    1. Ducks—Juvenile literature.   [1. Ducks]
I. Kessler, Leonard P., 1920—   ill.   II. Title.
III. Series
QL696.A52G64   1989   598.4'1   88-18073
ISBN 0-690-04780-0
ISBN 0-690-04782-7 (lib. bdg.)

    "A Harper trophy book."
    ISBN 0-06-445082-1

Ducks are water birds.

All day long they go in and out of the water. In and out, in and out.

No matter how many times they go into the water, ducks don't get wet. Ducks are waterproof.

Every duck is waterproof because it has an oil gland near its tail.

With its broad bill, the duck strokes this oil gland. Then it smears the oil over its feathers. This is called preening.

Ducks spend hours preening themselves. That is how they keep their feathers covered with oil.

Their feathers do not get wet because oil and water do not mix. Water rolls right off the oily feathers.

You can prove this for yourself.
Find some bird feathers in the woods or in a park.
Sprinkle water on one of the feathers. It will get
wet, because most bird feathers are not waterproof.

Dip your fingers in salad oil. Then pull another feather through them. Do this two or three times. Now the feather is coated with oil.

Sprinkle water on the oiled feather. The oiled feather will not get wet, because oil and water do not mix.

If you can't find any bird feathers, you can do another experiment to show that oil and water do not mix.

Take two brown paper bags. Smear some salad oil on one. Sprinkle water over both bags. The oiled paper bag will not get wet, because oil and water do not mix.

In the same way, water cannot get through the oil on the feathers of a duck.

9

Ducks spend most of their time in the water. They splash around in puddles and ponds, in swamps and shallow streams. They tip up in ditches and creeks. You can see ducks tipping their heads under the water and tipping their tails up in the air.

When ducks dabble in the water this way, they are searching for food. Their webbed feet paddle fast as they tug waterweeds with their broad bills.

Pintail ducks and mallards search through the water for pond grass and wild rice, for seeds and insects.

Blue-winged teals dip for wild rice and insects, clams, crayfish, and crabs.

Shoveler ducks waddle in and out of shallow water.
They shovel up mud and strain it for seeds and tiny
water plants. They scoop up water and strain it for
insects and shrimp.

Wood ducks look for water plants. They munch duckweeds and grass seeds, wild rice, water lily seeds, acorns, and hickory nuts.

Many ducks are expert divers.

Some ducks can dive to the bottom of very deep lakes.

They can dive down 100 feet. This is as deep as a ten-story building is high.

They can swim under water for 300 feet—the length of a city block. When they come up for air, they are dry.

Canvasbacks and scaups dive for wild celery and shellfish.

Harlequin ducks dive for insects and fish.

So do the buffleheads.

Mergansers dive for large fish. With its saw-edged bill, a merganser can catch and hold on to a slippery salmon or trout.

Ducks must find their food in the water or along the shores of lakes and ponds.

When the weather gets cold, the rivers and marshes, ponds and lakes are covered with ice.

When the water freezes, crabs and crayfish, duckweeds and pond weeds and all the fish are beneath the ice. Ducks cannot reach this good food.

Then the ducks leave the far north.

They fly southward to open water where they can find food.

Southward fly the dabbling ducks—

and the pintails,

the mallards

and the wood ducks.

the teals and the shovelers,

Southward fly the diving ducks—

the canvasbacks and scaups,

the harlequins and buffleheads,

the mergansers.

Southward, at 50, 60, 70 miles an hour—as fast as
a fast automobile—fly the ducks.

Southward to open water and good duck food fly the ducks. They may fly through sunshine or storm clouds. They may fly through buffeting winds and slanting rain. And the raindrops roll right off their backs.

If they fly over your house, you may be sure you will see them again next fall. Ducks travel the same route, or flyway, year after year. Sometimes they fly in a V formation. The leader flies at the point of the V, and the other ducks fan out behind.

When the ducks fly low, you may be able to see them clearly. You may be able to hear the hiss and whistle of the wind as it slips off their oiled feathers. You may be able to hear the heavy thumping of their powerful wings.

But when the ducks fly very high, you will not be able to hear them or to see a single duck clearly. You will know that the ducks are passing overhead only when you see a V in the sky that looks like a faint wisp of smoke.

You will know the ducks are flying southward for the winter.

When spring comes, the ducks will return.

They will fly north to dabble and dive in the rivers and lakes, in the ponds and marshes.

They will fly back to open water and good duck food.

They will fly back north through blustering winds and spring rains.

And they will always be dry—because ducks don't get wet.